T5-DHI-075

YOUR
**POCKET
THERAPIST**

# WHEN YOUR PARTNER WANTS TO LEAVE

*How to sort out your feelings
and plan for the future*

Dr. David B. Hawkins, ACSW, Ph.D.

*"Love is*

*not love*

*until love's*

*vulnerable."*

—THEODORE ROETHKE

Victor is an imprint of
Cook Communications Ministries, Colorado Springs, Colorado 80918
Cook Communications, Paris, Ontario
Kingsway Communications, Eastbourne, England

WHEN YOUR PARTNER WANTS TO LEAVE
© 2001 by David B. Hawkins

All rights reserved. No part of this book may be reproduced without written permission, except for brief quotations in books and critical reviews. For information, write Cook Communications Ministries, 4050 Lee Vance View, Colorado Springs, Colorado 80918.

ISBN: 0-78143-470-X
First Printing, 2001
Printed in the United States of America

Editors: Greg Clouse, Craig Bubeck
Cover & Interior Design: Global Images and iDesignEtc.

Scripture quotations are taken from the *Holy Bible: New International Version*®.
Copyright © 1973, 1978, 1984 by International Bible Society. Used by permission of Zondervan Publishing House. All rights reserved.

# ABOUT THE AUTHOR

A licensed clinical psychologist trained in the fields of social work and clinical psychology, Dr. David B. Hawkins, ACSW, Ph.D., has been in private practice for more than twenty years and specializes in domestic violence, adult and family issues, and marriage enrichment. Based in Longview, Washington, he is a certified domestic violence perpetrator treatment provider, certified forensic examiner, and a spiritual director. He also is a member of the National Association of Social Workers, Academy of Forensic Examiners, and the American Psychological Association. The author of several other books, including *See Dick and Jane Grow Up* (ISBN: 0-78143-498-X), David

cohosts a weekly radio program entitled "Experiencing Family," and was the host of an award-winning community television program called "Right Where You Live." He has been married to his wife, Diane (a nurse practitioner) for more than twenty-five years, and they have two grown sons. He enjoys snow and water skiing, hiking, kayaking, and running in recreational races in his free time.

# INTRODUCTION

The fact that you have picked up this **Your Pocket Therapist** booklet suggests that you may be experiencing one of the most serious crises of your life. Unfortunately you are not alone. Every day hundreds of couples face the demise of their relationship because one of them has found someone else or feels that he or she has "fallen out of love" with the partner. All too often the spouse did not see the crisis coming. Perhaps this describes what has happened to you. You knew things weren't perfect, but they didn't seem bad enough to warrant a termination of the relationship.

"I didn't see it coming," Susan said tearfully. "I thought things were going pretty well. Oh, sure, we've had our troubles. Who hasn't? But I still love him, even after what he's done. My friends tell me I shouldn't put up with him, but I don't want to give up thirteen years of marriage."

She continued to tell her story—one that I have heard hundreds of times, it seems with increased frequency. Though every story has its differences, many poignant features are the same.

Susan told me how she had learned that her husband had been seeing another woman. Brad didn't deny what she had accidentally found out. In fact, he proclaimed rather coldly that he had been involved with someone else for several months. He brazenly claimed he no longer loved Susan and was considering a divorce.

Susan felt like a bomb had been dropped on her chest. In fact, she had trouble catching her breath. While Brad sat there as if nothing were wrong, she felt anxiety pulse through her body. *This cannot be happening,* she thought. *Our marriage will be okay. He is just having a mid-life crisis.* She grasped for hope that things were not as bad as they seemed. Her attempts to get him to talk about it brought no response. Apparently he had been thinking about this for a while and had already made a choice that would severely impact their relationship and family.

"LOVE IS PATIENT, LOVE IS KIND. IT DOES NOT ENVY, IT DOES NOT BOAST, IT IS NOT PROUD. IT IS NOT RUDE, IT IS NOT SELF-SEEKING, IT IS NOT EASILY ANGERED, IT KEEPS NO RECORD OF WRONGS."

—*1 Corinthians 13:4-5*

In total despair Susan called their pastor. He agreed to come right over, though Brad made it clear that he would not meet with him. His decision reinforced how alone she felt. They had shared a relationship with the pastor and the church, but that apparently was over now. Christian values, a shared faith—none of that seemed to matter now. Brad was hardened and cold. He was a man she hardly knew anymore.

# DISPOSABLE RELATIONSHIPS

Thirteen years, and all Brad could say was that he had been out of love with Susan for a few years. How could this be? How could she not know what was happening? All of these questions raced through her mind, and they should enter our minds as well. You see, this is representative of not just a crisis for Brad and Susan, but for our entire society.

We all know that razors are disposable, as are paper plates and ballpoint pens—but relationships? What ever happened to the word *commitment?* What happened to "through good times and bad, for better or worse?" It sometimes seems we have reached a point where the vows ought to read, "Until things no longer work out between us." Certainly we can all agree that God made marriage to be a binding, permanent relationship; but we live in a fallen world, and we humans will falter.

Consequently, when we bind ourselves to another emotionally, physically, and yes, even spiritually, we cannot unbind ourselves easily. Even a spouse like Brad, who has left or is threatening to leave, cannot simply extricate himself from a union with a wish and a prayer. It is not that easy for either party. We have been created such that we bind our lives together like a rope with many strands. When a relationship comes apart, many strands remain intact, keeping a link to that other person. That, among other things, is what causes so much pain. Here you are, strongly attached to your spouse, who has tragically broken or ignored his or her bonds to you. He or she is prepared; you are not. You are left to pick up the fragments of your life. While you certainly are capable of doing that, you must first honor the significant pain you are experiencing. Your pain is a testimony to the depth of your love for your spouse. Your pain speaks to the many strands of your life that have become inextricably bound up with this significant person in your life.

Few circumstances in life leave one as hopeless and helpless as when a spouse seems determined to leave. Few events can pierce the heart like that of betrayal. I have seen individuals wracked with suicidal feelings because their reason for living was caught up in their intimate relationship with their spouse. When their spouse threw them away, they felt like disappearing themselves. I have seen individuals so confused they were unable to work, sleep, or even eat because of the chaos created by this loss in their life. The moral of the story is that when we marry, we all become bound together with our spouse, and we will not be able to let go easily. Nor should we be able to let go easily. Intimacy created is not easily broken. Our hearts are not easily mended. This type of wound runs deep and lasts long.

To be abandoned is one of our primitive fears. Many have experienced this in one form or another as children, and this new catastrophe re-creates an earlier trauma. For all of us, however, no matter what our backgrounds hold, rejection is very painful. To be "dumped" is one of the worst feelings that we can have. To be replaced for the affections of another is too painful to bear. No one, no matter how close a friend, can completely soothe the wounded soul set adrift by a spouse who wants to leave. Your pain is legitimate, and suffering is your right for the time being. While I do not advise that you set up camp there, you will be in emotional distress until the crisis subsides. We will talk more about how to survive this emotional distress as we move through this booklet together.

Let's look at another example of how this problem can happen, while we also look closely for the promise of healing that is ours if we are open to it.

# CAROLINE

Caroline and Jeffrey had been married for a few years. They had resisted marriage at first, but they finally "made the leap" and committed to each other. For the first year or so, it hadn't seemed to make much difference in their relationship. Marriage was more or less a formality. Little did Caroline know, however, that other events were happening that would profoundly impact their relationship.

Caroline had an experience strikingly similar to Susan's. One afternoon she was innocently looking through her husband's truck for something when she happened upon a number of feminine articles not belonging to her. Of course she immediately panicked, wondering what this could mean for their marriage. Wild thoughts ran through her mind while she desperately tried to regain control of her obsessive thinking. Every possible scenario of deceit passed through her mind before she was able to talk things out with Jeffrey.

When confronted, at first Jeffrey vehemently denied any knowledge of the articles or wrongdoing. He was indignant that his fidelity to her was being questioned. His rage confused her. Part of her felt relief that perhaps this was all a cruel misunderstanding. Perhaps he *was* faithful and she was free from any danger. But what if his protests were part of a masquerade to keep himself out of trouble? Was he trying to make her crazy? The evidence was right there in plain sight. While he protested loudly and effectively caused her to back off, the evidence was overwhelming. In an instant their relationship went from trust to distrust, from happiness to despair. She could not dismiss her doubts as quickly as he would have liked.

Caroline continued to quiz Jeffrey. She had a thousand questions, and he was impatient with her. She challenged him with the obvious facts before her, and the impossibility that they did not involve him in some way. Yet he pleaded innocence. He claimed that this was an explainable mistake. Perhaps the articles belonged to his business partners' wife—the partner had used his truck the week before.

Unknown to Caroline, Jeffrey had been unhappy in their relationship for a long time. He had decided to find comfort with other women. The truth was that this was not his first indiscretion. He had been having a series of affairs as a way to cope with his inner struggles, partly having to do with their relationship, partly having to do with stress in his business. He had been struggling with his double life and the guilt of his secret sin, but he feared confronting her.

Jeffrey was in a difficult spot. The more he lied, the further he felt trapped in his duplicity. He had created a double life and felt too insecure to change any part of it. Emotionally he felt too weak to let go of his wife, but he also felt that he couldn't let go of the comfort he found with other women. He knew in his heart that he wanted to leave, but feared making the change. If only there was a way to ease into the separation, he thought. But while that would ease his guilt regarding his actions of betrayal to Caroline, it would do little to ease the guilt of his moral failures. He knew that he had violated Caroline and had failed to live up to the standards of his Christian values. He could identify with the psalmist who, when talking about secret sin, said, *"When I kept silent my bones wasted away through my groaning all day long. For day and night your hand was heavy upon me"* (Psalm 32:3-4).

# CARL

It may be tempting to believe that only men are unfaithful and have the desire to escape committed relationships. However, this is not the case. Women also often choose to leave relationships or engage in infidelity. They too become dissatisfied and start to look around for some external way of easing their inner tension. Seeking the excitement of a new relationship is often one of the first measures people attempt, hoping to fulfill something missing inside. Women have this dilemma as often as men, as is illustrated in the following story.

Carl is an example of a man who was devoted to his wife. With two young children, a new home, and a budding career, he thought everything was fine. They were often looked upon by friends at church and the tennis club as being the perfect couple. He maintained the illusion that things were fine until his wife, Sherrie, came to him one evening, announcing that she was moving out.

"Moving out? You've got to be kidding! What is going on?" he asked incredulously. "I don't understand. We have everything any couple could want. You have no idea what you would be giving up!"

Sherrie was in tears. She had dreaded this moment and had been preparing to tell Carl for weeks. There was never a right time to announce something like this.

"It's no use, Carl. I don't think I love you anymore, and I feel hemmed in here. I need to be on my own for a while."

"What does that mean?" He became increasingly angry. "You can't just walk up to me and your two kids and say that you need a little time away. Wouldn't we all like a break now and then?"

"Listen, Carl. There's no reason to yell at me. I've been thinking about this for a long time. I don't know how I feel about anything anymore. Everybody needs something from me, and I feel as if I'm being pulled apart. I don't know who I am. I have to figure out what I think."

Carl panicked. He had no idea that it had come down to this. He knew that their relationship had been tense of late . . . even cold, but he never thought Sherrie would walk out on him and their kids. In desperation he made more accusations.

"So tell me the truth. Is there someone else? There must be someone else for you to be acting this way. This is not like you. This is crazy!"

"No, there is no one else," Sherrie said. "And lower your voice, please. The kids do not need to be a part of this. And as far as another relationship, that is the last thing I want right now. I don't need anyone else pulling me in another direction. I told you, I'm trying to figure out what I think."

Carl tried to press her for more specifics, seeking some sign that this was just a bluff; but finally he just walked out of the room. He tried to collect himself, but found that he really felt terrified of Sherrie leaving him. All of the sudden he was filled with guilt over the way the way he'd been taking her for granted. Random thoughts sped through his mind. Just as quickly as he felt guilt, however, he justified his behavior and felt angry with her for needing her "space."

Sherrie, meanwhile, sat down in their family room and tried to consider the full magnitude of what she was doing. She wondered if Carl was right. What gave her the right to selfishly pursue her wishes? And what would happen if she decided to leave the kids with Carl? What would their family and friends think? Was she leaving a bad situation only to find something worse on her own? There were no easy answers, and friends gave differing opinions that were absolutely no help. They were on their own to sort this one out.

# Similarities and Differences

Scenarios similar to these happen every day in homes all over the world. Every few minutes some family is disrupted by someone who feels compelled to seek comfort with someone else, or another who needs to rediscover individuality. Many relationships are disrupted because the spark has been replaced by the desperate hope that love can be found somewhere else.

Every case bears its own consequences to these actions. Families are divided. Children are confused and devastated. Marriages are often ruined, only to have destructive patterns repeat themselves in the future. We cannot run from ourselves.

Sometimes, however, separations lead to changes in a relationship that can rescue it from absolute disaster. For this salvation, however, the separation must be executed with the care and skill of a surgeon. When done in the right way, the odds of saving the relationship increase greatly. That is one of the primary reasons for writing this booklet: to save a relationship when your spouse wants to leave!

*When Your Partner Wants to Leave* is a booklet filled with the darkness of reality, as well as the brightness of hope. As an experienced psychologist who has worked with hundreds of couples in these dire circumstances, I have seen healing come to the most distraught and painful situation imaginable. I have seen couples move from the brink of disaster, filled with self-centered pursuits, back to sacrificial love. I have watched as couples who felt angry and hopeless rekindled the dying embers and found love again. It can happen for you too.

This booklet is about a complex topic. There are no easy answers. Let's try to understand why spouses leave and what can be done to prevent it from happening. Let's learn about how to save things once it *has* happened. Though things may look bleak at this moment, it is not time to abandon ship. Maintain the course, and get out the map for new directions.

"WE SHOULD NOT LET OUR
FEARS HOLD US BACK FROM
PURSUING OUR HOPES."

— *John F. Kennedy*

# *Phase 1*
## LEAVING

Why do so many want to leave their relationship? What is it that makes the grass look so much greener across the street? The divorce rate hovers around 50 percent, and second marriages do not fare much better. (And these figures do not even take into consideration all the relationships that have reached intimacy, but fall short of taking the step of a marriage commitment.) Countless couples seem to be stable only to have one spouse become intensely dissatisfied.

I have long believed that maintaining a healthy relationship is the most difficult task that we will ever undertake. I believe it is more difficult than being a parent, and we all know how terrifying it is trying to raise a healthy child. Keeping a relationship healthy is even more daunting. So many odds work against us it is surprising we can keep love alive at all. Pressures from within and without tempt us to let things simply fall apart. When we don't vigilantly protect this fragile and delicate organism that we are growing, it will surely die. Too often, it does just that.

There are many ways both men and women choose to leave a relationship. One of them, which we will discuss in depth later, is unfaithfulness. While this seems to be the easiest way to leave an unwanted relationship, it is also the most devastating. In working with couples, I have seen little that is more painful than infidelity. If they knew the utter destruction that would take place, would they still make the same choices?

But let's set our judgments aside for the moment and look at some of the many reasons a spouse chooses to leave. As we do this, it is best to be as broad-minded as possible, in spite of the intense feelings and vengeful fantasies we may have. Beneath these surface feelings are probably much hurt and grief. These are also the feelings that will ultimately help you heal.

***Boredom:*** One of the primary reasons a spouse chooses to leave is because the relationship has become mundane. Life has become a series of tasks to be done, dishes to be washed, and bills to be paid. Little excitement is left for the spouse in turmoil. You know how it goes—life is filled with all the little things that preoccupy our minds. One obligation here, one crisis there. Time gets filled with the routine, leaving little room for anything else.

Wait a minute, you might say. Relationships are not always filled with romance and roses. The spark can't flame all the time. You might be thinking that the dissatisfied spouse should just get a grip and grow up. The fun times are over, and responsibilities need attention.

Certainly there is some truth to this. *Within each of us, however, is the desire to feel admired, loved, and excited about our relationship.* Too many relationships become mired in the day-in, day-out activities of work, shopping, taking the kids to soccer, and then dragging off to bed. Little time or energy is left for romance. In due time, someone will tire of the boredom and begin to long for more.

If you watch many couples closely, you'll notice conversation filled with perfunctory messages. "Don't forget to pay the heating bill today. . . . Can you pick up Charity from her piano lessons? . . .Would you pick up some milk on your way home tonight? . . .We need to make sure that the lawn gets mowed before it goes to pasture." Perhaps you recognize this way of interacting in your relationship.

On and on it goes; except then it takes a critical turn. After a while you might hear something like, "Why didn't you pick up my clothes from the dry cleaners like I asked? . . . Could you please clear your plate from the table? . . . Do you have to spend so much on your lunches? . . . Why do you leave your hair to clog up the drain?" When conversation is reduced to such barbs, the lifeblood of affection drains out of the relationship.

Both partners begin dying inside, hardly noticing that they are taking one another for granted. No one shouts, "Stop!" No one announces that both need to change the way they live and talk to one another. No one notices that love is leaving until one says those tragic words, "I'm leaving." All of the sudden, there is a resounding wake-up call.

Desires to seek more from the relationship may be difficult for either party to put into words. Fearing hurt feelings, many choose instead to let resentment smolder and increase under the surface. What began as boredom and an unspoken need for greater intimacy ultimately leads to resentment. Can you see any patterns here that may fit your situation? If so, take a moment to write down what you consider may be relevant to your relationship. Keeping a journal to record your reactions may be helpful as you work through this booklet.

**_Resentment:_** Many couples do not know exactly what they need, let alone _how_ to get their needs met. How do we ask for what we need? How do we even figure out what we need? These are the first steps in what is usually a very difficult task for most people. When attempts to have needs met within the relationship fail, a spouse may choose to look outside the relationship for satisfaction. Often tremendously ambivalent and guilt- ridden about such actions, a discontented spouse will take desperate action when the pain reaches a certain threshold. This often seems easier than working at rebuilding the current relationship. _Almost always it is meeting a legitimate need in an illegitimate way._

Resentment is unresolved anger, like a cancer eroding the health of a relationship. We all know what it feels like. To some, it is a sinking feeling in the pit of their stomachs, often accompanied by increasingly meanspirited thoughts regarding the object of their ill will. For others it may be outright rage percolating to the surface, with teeth clenched, fists tightened, and every muscle in the body rigid with tension.

Resentment often takes one of two forms. The first is outright conflict that is not resolved. The anger and hostility are constant companions in the relationship, to the point where the couple may feel like they no longer know one another. Their only contact is arguments, fights, and cold war. In this case issues are not resolved, intimacy is lost, and emotional distance will be followed by a physical departure. They have failed to heed Paul's words to _"Let no unwholesome talk come out of your mouths, but only what is helpful for building others up according to their needs" (Eph. 4:29)._ Resentment builds upon resentment, and bitterness prevails. Couples who are alert and conscious to these changes can see the breakdown happening and make some kind of effort to avert disaster.

The second pattern of resentment is the quiet, distant, smoldering relationship. One spouse—for the sake of discussion, let's say the wife—tires of having her feelings misunderstood. Discouraged, and perhaps depressed, she may go through the motions of companionship, but be vacant emotionally. Her fantasies are filled with leaving. She may fantasize a way out without wreaking havoc on her spouse and others involved. For many these detached relationships can go on for years without either party really telling the other the truth about the way things are. Ultimately, however, the strain of keeping a lid on things finally takes its toll, and she makes the move.

_**The Affair:**_ Of course this topic would not be complete without discussing one of the major reasons that a spouse wants to leave: the other woman or man. What pain, grief, and devastation are caused by an affair ironically initiated to obtain relief! Finding comfort in a friend too often leads to more than friendship. For most it was never planned. They never intended to hurt their spouse.

Words are never adequate in fully explaining how an affair happens. Rationalization does not comfort the wounded heart of the spouse whose trust has been shattered. The hard reality is that an affair is no less than an intense violation of the soul. An intruder has entered the sacred relationship, and the spiritual union has been ripped apart. Three people have occupied a space designed for only two.

Once the affair has been found out, blame flies fast, furious—and far. The lines are drawn: the dumper and the dumpee, the wrong and the right, and friends and family choose sides. The act of betrayal ushers in a judgment day with no doubt of the guilt of the accused. The betrayer is seen as totally at fault, irredeemable, and less than human for what he or she has done. But let's look a little deeper.

The wronged parties can react with hurt and anger, giving full force to whatever pent-up hostilities have accumulated over the years. On the other hand, the wronged may take on the full burden of the problem, wondering what could have been done differently so this would not have happened. They scrutinize their character for any minute flaw that could explain this. "I must have caused it by some form of inadequacy," they will reason. What often follows is intense self-punishment. Healing is often slow and torturous, if the relationship survives at all. It is very difficult to set aside judgment and focus on the problems that each party brought to the relational turmoil.

Affairs surely can be the destructive damage of one ruthless, insensitive individual. I have seen that happen many times. Affairs are often, however, the result of long-standing problems in the relationship. They may occur partially because of the relationship issues we have discussed, namely boredom and resentment. They may also occur because of personality factors of the unfaithful, such as lack of commitment, a search for freedom, or a way out of the relationship. It is usually a symptom of deeper problems, both within the relationship and within the person. The gentle, listening ear of another is often quite seductive to the lonely person who has nursed a grudge for a while.

This is not to justify what has happened. *Affairs are never a way to resolve relational problems.* Having said that, rarely do I see situations where one party is totally to blame. If you find yourself in this excruciating situation, consider what may have been happening in the relationship that can help explain your current circumstances. Such analysis is difficult in this stressful situation, but it is necessary for your healing—with or without your spouse.

*The Unfulfilled Life:* Many individuals who have been unable to find personal stability and satisfaction will be unable to sustain stability and satisfaction as part of a marriage relationship. In the field of psychology, these issues are called *character problems.* From a Christian perspective, this often occurs when we have failed to find our true identity and spiritual gifts. We are not utilizing our spiritual gifts to build up the church body, and thus be encouraged ourselves (Rom. 12:3-8).

Consider the following situation. Julie is a legal secretary who has worked hard at her career. Prior to reaching a prestigious position in a prominent law firm, she felt insecure about herself, struggling with many unfinished emotional problems from childhood. Her career had masked these problems and given her a façade of contentment. When she was basking in the recognition that her job brought her, she did not have to face the personal fires that had never been put to rest. They simply smoldered below the surface, waiting for a chance to flame up.

Her marriage to Randy blossomed at first. They were not long into their relationship, however, when both began to sense her useless attempts to escape from her past. She did not want to spend much time at home and seemed anxious in the domestic role. While her fast-paced lifestyle was not a problem in their early years, now with two young children, Randy wanted more out of their relationship and family life.

Julie, on the other hand, felt more trapped by her family and sought more avenues of escape. Shopping and partying were ways for her to cope with inner restlessness. When active with her friends, career, and shopping, she was relatively content. Tension began to develop, however, when Randy wanted to slow down their lives and focus more on their family. He was ready to give up the late nights and simplify their lives. He wanted to anchor their family in a church and develop their spiritual lives. She was not on the same page at all. Stillness and quiet were the perfect kindling for the inner fires that she did not want to face. A crisis loomed in their future.

Julie complained of her unfulfilled life, *not to be confused with her filled life.* And she projected her dissatisfaction upon her husband. Julie labeled Randy's desire for tranquility and stability as boredom. She called his desire for spiritual depth "goody two shoes." Her attitude was clear: "You go ahead and deal with your religious cravings—go to church. Just don't expect me to do it. I'm too young for that."

Julie's story is but one example of the unfulfilled life that seeks satisfaction from external sources, rather than by God's healing of the real issues from within. It is often tempting to look for the quick fix outside of ourselves than to look for emotional and spiritual problems that need to be addressed.

_**Power and Control:**_ Some circumstances exist in which a spouse ought to temporarily leave. There are situations where one spouse's individuality and sense of self is at risk of being swallowed by another's need to control.

You may know what I am referring to here. It is quite common for one person in the relationship to want to dominate the spouse. Such an individual has often been raised in an environment where he or she was controlled, thus having effectively learned to control as well. _Life for these people means having power and control._ They want life to exist on their terms, and when things do not go their way, they will act in some manner to regain control.

Control can start in a most subtle way. It can be disguised in the form of "caring." For example, the controller may be "concerned" about the spouse's choice of friends and begins making derogatory comments about them. Feeling threatened, the spouse is unable to talk about the problem any other way. Feelings of fear are thus transformed into controlling behaviors.

Or perhaps it will start over the use of money. One may become excessively adamant about how money should be spent. So the spouse's taste is required to conform to the other's desires. Again, the real issue is control. Submission and sensitivity to each other's needs, as called for in Ephesians 5, is sorely lacking. Instead, financial decisions are always one-sided.

This kind of suffocation will almost always lead to the breakdown of the relationship and cause one person to want to leave. A healthy relationship is based on equality, in which two people come together with different desires and needs. While these differences cause tension at times, they are also the qualities that create an exciting energy. Consider how boring it would be if everyone were exactly the same. It would be like a world without color, free from tension perhaps, but also incredibly boring. If your spouse wants out, ask yourself if you have been too controlling. Look at how you have made your voice heard when it comes to extra money, dress, friends and work habits. How do you as a couple make decisions affecting both of you? Are both of you able to share your feelings freely? Ask your spouse if he or she feels complete freedom to be honest. However, be warned: do this only if you are willing to deal with complete honesty!

***Spiritual Poverty:*** Perhaps the most important reason for the breakup of any relationship is when the spiritual union has been broken. Relationships are not comprised only of passion, erotic feelings, and emotion. They are also spiritual in nature, comprised of self-giving, sacrificial, *agape* love. That love, as we all realize at some point, cannot be generated with white-knuckled, gritty determination. It does not come from within, no matter how strong and stubborn we are. Efforts to try to generate it on our own will lead to utter frustration. Rather, it is a gift from God, and it comes from our complete surrender to Him.

Spiritual poverty is a terrible thing. Perhaps you can relate to the barren place that Alcoholic Anonymous programs call "self-will run riot." We talk a lot about having a strong self-concept, positive self-confidence, and self-determination. But sooner or later we come to the end of the road—of self-importance, that is—and realize that we need a power greater than ourselves.

Such power can only come from the one true source of spiritual strength: God's Holy Spirit, dwelling within a believer. It's a hard reality, but we have to accept that—despite the common wisdom of our world—we really don't have sufficient power within to sate our spiritual needs. Indeed, we must come to see that our self-driven personality has succeeded in only creating destruction. This is notoriously a significant cause for relationships crashing to the bottom.

You may be in a broken relationship today because you or your spouse has become self-absorbed in a destructive way. Your spouse may have become obsessed with the advancement of the self, according to worldly standards. If he or she has taken that road, emptiness inevitably lies ahead, and you may be the recipient of the frustration that comes of a meaningless existence. Unable to find peace with one's self and God, there cannot very well be peace with you.

# Phase 2
## DEALING WITH THE CRISIS

Before we go on to deal with repairing a relationship, it may help to look at what part relationships play in our lives. For most of us, our lives revolve around our relationships. They are the very fabric of life. When our relationships are not going well, we are not doing well. When we are faced with a spouse who wants out of the relationship, who wants to disrupt our entire lives, we will experience a serious crisis. *A crisis, by definition, is any situation which we are not prepared to manage.* We have not read any books about the problem ahead of time and have not determined the most effective way to cope. Because of this, many handle the situation as if they are throwing gas on a fire that is threatening to burn their home. But obviously, fanning the flames, so to speak, only serves to destroy more of what is important to you. Thankfully, there is a better way. Let's talk about it.

How do you manage this crisis? My suggestions are based on the premise that you want to restore the relationship. *I also want to state strongly that most often the relationship can be saved.* But feelings must be contained and managed. It is my experience that after initial reactions of disbelief, leading to feelings of rage and hurt, come feelings of fear. Most likely you do not really want to lose your spouse, and this crisis is a wake-up call signaling a needed change in the relationship. Here, then, are a few coping strategies to help stabilize and possibly restore the relationship. It is important to remember that following these simple guidelines will not fix the problems that created the crisis; however, they will greatly increase the odds of your relationship working out again after the crisis subsides.

***Don't Panic:*** "Yeah, sure," you reply. "Easy for you to say." This is obviously much easier said than done. Again, by definition a crisis is something we are not prepared to handle, and it is usually quite disorienting. In a state of disorientation and confusion, many overreact or act in ways contrary to their best interests. Most of us tend to have knee-jerk reactions that only make matters worse. We are not thinking clearly, and so we make poor choices.

Examples of overreaction include becoming violent and pushing your spouse further away. "If you want to leave," you reason, "then you can totally leave . . . and never return." You may be tempted to say, "If you leave, just go ahead and get a divorce. I'm not going to live with a separation." Of course, this response (possibly attempted manipulation) is not reasonable and does not stem from thoughtful consideration of the problem. Your spouse may really need some space, or is determined to get some space; and making threats will not be helpful. You will just look more desperate and lose respect in his or her eyes. That is *not* how you want to be seen at a time like this. So, try not to panic. Take time to collect yourself before taking any drastic actions.

This is a time, obviously, for prayer. It is a time when you will need abundant doses of the peace of God that passes understanding. It is a time to cry out to God for wisdom and understanding. Thankfully we have the promise, *"If you accept my words and store up my commands within you, turning your ear to wisdom and applying your heart to understanding, and if you call out for insight and cry aloud for understanding, and if you look for it as silver and search for it as for hidden treasure, then you will understand the fear of the Lord and find the knowledge of God" (Prov. 2:1-5).* In this disorienting time the Lord will be there to help you sort things out.

Another panic reaction is worth mentioning. The opposite reaction of kicking your spouse out is begging him or her to stay. You fear losing the loved one and start making promises to change anything and everything. This too causes loss of respect for you. If your spouse wants or needs to leave, you need to release! But do not grovel and demean yourself.

***Get Support:*** Consistent with the first suggestion is the strategy of seeking support. Hopefully you have a friend, pastor, or church family who can help you sort out your options. Caring friends at a time like this are like a rudder to a ship that has been set adrift. They will help you, if you will allow, to become centered as you look over the situation.

You will not be able to imagine right now how valuable their support will become to you. You will face times when you need them to help sort out the "craziness."

Ah, but you are not used to reaching out and asking for help, you say. Yes, crises force us to dig deep inside to find new ways of coping. Asking for help is one of those new tools you will need to keep the ship afloat. We all need help at times, and there is nothing wrong with that. In fact, not only is it natural, but it can be flattering for your friends to be asked to help you. Believe me, they will need you sometime in the future, and they will be glad to have some money in the bank that they can draw upon when the need arises.

***Let Your Spouse Go:*** This tool bears repeating because it is so important. "Let go?" you say. "But I have two hundred reasons for staying and dealing with the problem. There is so much that we'd be throwing away by separating—what we need is to pause, put our heads on straight, and take another look at the situation." *Yes, there are many reasons why your relationship should be saved; but clinging to it, or bickering with your spouse, will only push him or her further away.* (It can be helpful to *calmly* share some consequences of actions, but lecturing is rarely helpful.)

If your spouse really wants to leave (and the spouse wanting to leave is often more confused about this than the other may know), you must let it be so. Again, excessive anger, tears, clinging, or promises will only foster increasing disrespect. Please do not misunderstand. This does not mean that you simply act like you do not care. You do! But you are saying that you respect your spouse enough to allow him or her to choose. Your spouse will have second thoughts about this choice, and when that happens, you want to look healthy.

***Suggest a Period for Both to Evaluate the Relationship:*** Assuming that you have sought stabilizing support, and you have learned that life will not come to an end without your spouse, you can now suggest a framework in which you both can reevaluate your relationship. You have succeeded in not overreacting and pushing away, and perhaps he or she is willing to listen to a little bit of solid reason. So, make a very low-key proposal. Low-key is the important qualifier here. (In my experience, most spouses, though wanting to leave, still see the inherent wisdom of this proposal and are willing to try it.)

Your proposal has to be something that will alleviate the confusion for both of you. Remember that your spouse is not as sure about this as might have been portrayed. Moving out is a huge decision, and you can be sure that he or she is wondering about it in one way or another. So, you step up as the rational one who makes a reasonable proposal.

The proposal goes something like this: This will be a period of time when you have no or few expectations and demands of each other. *You are both free.* You are free to leave and free to stay. However, encourage your spouse, in that freedom, to step back and take an honest look at the relationship.

Ideally, set aside this time for reflection. Consider proposing 90 days during which you choose to reevaluate your relationship. During this time, both should agree to six things:

- to not engage in other relationships;
- to take no legal actions;
- to seek relationship counseling;
- to not talk about ending the relationship;
- to uphold the relationship in prayer; and
- to be separated, perhaps legally, if that is important to either of you.

Now, don't be surprised if your spouse refuses to enter into counseling. This is common. If that is the case, your spouse may at least agree to the other conditions. Ask if he or she will agree to meet with a Christian professional counselor at least once during the 90 days to talk about the relationship.

During this time, you both can take an honest look at the pros and cons of the relationship. Perhaps, surprisingly, when the conflict is lessened, you will both be able to see the strengths in the relationship that may be worth saving. If you engage in couples counseling, you can often restore the love and appreciation that once existed.

*Set Healthy Boundaries:* During this difficult time you do not have to sit and wait out the storm, watching your life dissolve around you. In fact, quite the opposite. You need to take constructive action. If your spouse is involved with someone else, he or she should not be involved with you. It is demeaning to all concerned if either is "having the cake and eating it too." Instead, set clear boundaries that cannot be misunderstood; for bad choices there necessarily must be repercussions.

You may find yourself in a situation where your spouse does not want to leave, yet also does not want to stay. The same boundaries apply here. He or she needs to be forced into making a choice. This firmness on your part will reveal the fabric of your integrity by standing firmly upon the requirement that your relationship will not continue with anything less than a total commitment to healthy change.

As you set these boundaries, you need to make it clear (if it is true) that you are committed to a healthy relationship. You will do your part to make the changes necessary for a healthy relationship. You can show your spouse your level of commitment by entering therapy, exercising, getting the right kind of nutrition, and tuning up your spiritual life. All of these things can only help you, at the same time making you more attractive in his or her eyes. But you must resolutely refuse to diminish your value by groveling or begging the one you love to stay; likewise, you must determine not to wait forever for a decision. Your spouse must decide to work with you for change, or leave.

***Decide to Attempt to Save the Relationship or to Dissolve it:*** If you have followed the steps recommended, you are in a position to honestly determine if the relationship can be saved. *What is needed is not a new relationship, but a renewed relationship.* Spouses who are committed to finding the lost passion are usually able to do so. While it may appear that the relationship is doomed, with some serious tuning it can be revitalized.

You will worry that "the feelings aren't there" that are needed to save the relationship. This is common, but it is not something on which to base a radical decision. You and your spouse can be assured that if you will follow some steps designed to revitalize your relationship, the feelings will return. Over 95 percent of couples who have chosen to "rekindle the fire" have succeeded. The spark of the relationship has simply been doused by conflict or neglect. Do not assume that the love, the commitment, the respect, and all the other emotions you have felt for each other are gone simply because the romantic feelings are not burning. They can be rekindled.

Sadly, sometimes the relationship cannot be restored. Your

spouse may be resolute in wanting out of the relationship and is unwilling to participate in the 90-day trial period. He or she may have decided to stay with the new partner. In that event you will need to seek counseling on how to cope with the loss of your love. While this is often crushing, there is life after the ending of a relationship.

***Choosing to End the Relationship:*** Something must be said for the weary one who has lost the ability, or desire, to remain in the muddled madness. Many of you have been *through it* too many times and are ready for a new beginning. When the hellish fires of rage diminish, you may think that starting over doesn't sound too bad—certainly not as bad as repeating old habits. What counsel is available for you?

First, and most obvious, *weigh out the issues.* What is the cost to you if this relationship dissolves? What are the benefits? How much of your self have you lost in these destructive games people play? What are you hearing God say to you? In spite of the counsel you receive to hang in there, do you feel that the toll is just too high. Only you can make that assessment, just as only you have to live with the repercussions of your decisions.

Second, as you are weighing out your options, *look for wise counsel.* Many are willing to give free advice. Some poor advice may even come from close friends or relatives. Talk to believers who have integrity and stability and aren't just planning vengeful attacks. The sweetness of revenge fades very quickly. Listen for the ring of truth—is the counsel biblical at its core? As you prayerfully consider your options, and seek godly wisdom, the answers will come.

Third, *start on your path toward healing*. A decision to end a relationship is a profoundly trying move. It saps your strength and jars your equilibrium. You may not simply rebound into a new life. It takes time to put a new life into motion. Take your time, and take care of yourself.

Fourth, *determine what part you have played in this difficult drama*. Part of your healing comes from learning about your past. It has been said that those who do not understand the past are destined to repeat it. So true. It is easy to blame all the relational ills on your spouse, but you can only play that game so long. You must keep house with yourself. Honesty will help you put things into perspective, helping you immensely in future relationships.

Fifth, *focus on the road ahead*. Your future does not have to be dictated by your past. Resist the temptation to project negativity onto your future. Learn all you can about yourself, including your failures, and weave it all into a new, creative tapestry. Enjoy the new adventure. Remember that *"in all things God works for the good of those who love him, who have been called according to his purpose" (Rom. 8:28)*. God is able to take the lemons of your life and make lemonade!

Finally, if you decide to travel alone you may find that this is not in keeping with your spouse's plans, who may want to bounce back and forth. He or she may try it alone, see the other side, and then come back for more with you. This is not a good situation. You've tried this and found how gut-wrenching it can be. You do not want any part of this Ping-Pong game.

***Keep the Faith:*** What in the world do you mean by keeping the faith? you may ask. First of all, it has been proven that those who have a spiritual faith will fare much better during the storms of life. But more fundamentally, we who are Christians can always rest in the hope that God is in control—the question is, do we have faith in that promise? The Bible is clear that storms will come for all of us, and in truth the best we can do is cling to our faith, believing that God will work everything out for good "for those who love [and trust in] Him" (Rom. 8:28). Indeed, those who know their Creator can see His invisible hand farther down the line. All trials can be character builders if you will let them . . . if you will trust in Him.

"NOW FAITH IS BEING
SURE OF WHAT WE HOPE FOR
AND CERTAIN OF WHAT
WE DO NOT SEE."

—*Hebrews 11: 1*

# *Phase 3*

# PREVENTION STRATEGIES FOR THE FUTURE

What you are going through, or have been through, is likely something you would rather never repeat. Trust, stability, and predictability are values that strike at the core of our being, and we do not fare well when they are challenged. Please take very good care of yourself in this crisis. Get help for yourself even if your spouse will not get help with you. Often when one seeks help, the other will soon follow. Here is a quick review of principles that I am sure you know, but they bear repeating to avert a similar crisis in the future.

*Communication:* Perhaps this word is overused, but it still speaks to the heart of what is probably missing when one wants to leave the relationship. By communication I do not simply mean sharing ones thoughts and feelings with the other, as important as that is. Rather, communication must also include real listening and understanding of your spouse. What drives him or her? What is important, and what may be missing from your relationship? When we do not feel understood, we will seek to be understood by others.

*Friendship:* Someone has said that friendship is the ability to feel at home with another, as well as the comfort in being able to be transparent with that person.

It is a special thing to have someone who will listen to you, understand you, and help you to understand yourself better.

This takes an atmosphere of caring, comfort, and trust. Judgments must be set aside if we want our spouse to feel free to be transparent. We are, in essence, saying that it is okay to be exactly who he or she is. When we feel that, we have arrived at home and will not want to leave.

Special care must be taken to create an environment where there is joy being in the presence of the other. Here we are relaxed and encouraged to be all that we are capable of being. This is true friendship and will keep the relationship stable.

***Shared Interest/Values:*** Couples who have reached this crisis have drifted apart. Invariably one will say he or she no longer feels close or connected to the spouse. Attempts to bridge the gaps have proven futile, and the expanse of the chasm now is too much to endure.

Those who are able to sustain intimacy over the years have developed shared interests and rituals that have meaning for them. It is not that they have to be together all the time—quite the contrary. Both spouses have found activities that are gratifying on their own. But they have built a solid bridge of experiences that are enjoyed by both, and practiced by both on a regular basis. The dryness of distance is not allowed to develop. When this begins to happen, one will alert the other of the need to spend quality time together, and thus add zest to the relationship.

But what about the couple who has lost the ability to find mutually gratifying activities? To them I say, renew your quest for the adventure of finding joy in the relationship again. You will need to commit yourselves to the 90-day experiment, with each being responsible for creating new, low-demand adventures that will bring the "juice" back into the relationship. Don't be afraid to try new things, to be silly and childlike again. Playfulness is an incredible antidote to a stale relationship. Many a relationship has experienced stagnation by the seriousness of adult life.

*__Humor:__* Don't take yourself too seriously. It can be summed up by saying, "The situation is desperate, but fortunately not serious." Stand back a few steps and notice that a 5-percent change in behaviors reflects a fifty percent change in feelings. Not a bad return on investment! A little medicine goes a long way.

Smile! Catch each other doing things worth complimenting. Loosen up and look for the good in each other. What you loved and appreciated about each other is still present, but eroded by years of distance, seriousness, resentment, and any number of other maladies afflicting your union. Make a list of all of the assets your spouse brings to the relationship. Remember back when you first met him or her. Why did you choose to enter into this relationship? More importantly, what caused you to choose to commit yourself? When you can recapture some of those feelings and observations, you can make deposits in the love account again. It has been overdrawn for some time and needs the deposits of attention, caring, complimenting, and old-fashioned kindness.

*__Seek Support:__* Do not go through these kinds of difficulties alone. Let down your pride and find a knowledgeable counselor who can guide you through your struggles to the other side.

It's been said that darkness cannot exist with the light. Or put another way, light overcomes darkness. What is kept in secret remains in the dark, and nothing grows in the dark. Sharing your struggles with others brings them into the light with fresh perspectives. Seek the support of someone who can help, and see if things don't change for the better.

You may be saying, "What if my spouse will not seek counseling with me?" That's okay. Go alone and get support for yourself. Seeking counseling will certainly affect your spouse. Change within one person always leads to changes in others. Try it and see what happens.

***Spiritual Humility:*** Finally, remember the source of your true strength does not lie in yourself. *"Blessed are the poor in spirit, for theirs is the kingdom of God" (Matt. 5:3).* We must always remember that we cannot find all the answers that we need within ourselves. This is, frankly, a lie perpetuated by many. While we are given clear and rational minds to use, the heart is also wicked and deceptive. We need a source of wisdom outside of ourselves—God.

So, let me encourage you to remain grounded in your faith. Seek godly wisdom through Scripture and the counsel of wise, Christian friends. Let this crisis be spiritually invigorating to you, driving you to realign yourself with godly values.

# CONCLUSION

It can be extremely painful when a spouse, whom you deeply care about, threatens to leave. Or perhaps worse yet, when he or she seeks comfort in the arms of another person. This can be absolutely devastating to your self-esteem and to the relationship. Questions race through your mind about what you have done wrong. Temptations to bombard yourself with blame are common. Temptations to attack your spouse verbally may also be overwhelming. But these tactics lead nowhere.

If this crisis has happened to you, try to follow some of the steps presented in this booklet. It is a healthy place to start. If you will take the necessary steps toward healing, there is a good chance that your relationship will rise from the ashes of despair to become stronger than ever. It is hard to envision that now, but believe Jesus' encouraging words: "with God all things are possible" (Matt. 19:26).

No matter what the outcome, be careful not to denigrate yourself. Take responsibility where appropriate, and grow from the situation—that's the beginning of what Scripture calls repentance. Work hard at not holding a flaming grudge against your spouse—that's the beginning of what Scripture calls forgiveness. That seed of resentment will only grow and contaminate you from within. Try to remember that life is like a flowing river of God's will. You can move in new directions within His will, becoming stronger each step of the way. In these hard times, take care of yourself!

# SHARE YOUR STORY

Throughout the development of this book series, we have been introduced to many exceptional individuals. We are interested in hearing your stories. We want to share your experiences so that we in turn can share them with others. Please send your thoughts to:

**Your Pocket Therapist**
Dr. David B. Hawkins
1801 First Avenue, Suite 3B
Longview, WA 98632
(360) 425-3854

Dr. Hawkins has established an exciting web site that offers encouragement for families. The site features help on family issues, links to other relevant sites, and information about setting up seminars or speaking engagements.

Visit his ministry at www.InCourageMinistry.com.

# RECOMMENDED READING

Arp, David and Claudia. *Ten Great Dates to Revitalize Your Marriage.* Zondervan Publishing Company, 1997.

Gray, John. *Men, Women, and Relationships.* Harper, 1996.

Powell, John. *Why Am I Afraid to Tell You Who I Am.* Argus Communications, 1967.

Rankin, Howard. *Ten Steps to a Great Relationship.* Stepwise Printing, 1998.

Smalley, Gary and John Trent. *The Language of Love.* Focus on the Family Publishing, 1988.

White, Ben. *The 100 Best Ways to Stay Together.* Dell Publishing Company, 1998.